LEARN ABOUT SEEDS

by Golriz Golkar

Published by The Child's World®
1980 Lookout Drive • Mankato, MN 56003-1705
800-599-READ • www.childsworld.com

Design Elements: Shutterstock Images
Photographs ©: iStockphoto, cover (sprout), 1 (sprout); Shutterstock Images, cover (jar), 1 (jar), 4 (paper towels), 4 (right seeds), 9, 13, 14, 17, 19, 23; Pavel Vinnik/Shutterstock Images, 4 (left seeds); Rick Orndorf, 5, 6; Shyripa Alexandr/Shutterstock Images, 10; Adriana Nikolova/Shutterstock Images, 20

ISBN 9781503832176
LCCN 2018962830

Printed in the United States of America
PA02420

About the Author

Golriz Golkar is a teacher and children's author who lives in Nice, France. She enjoys cooking, traveling, and looking for ladybugs on nature walks.

TABLE OF CONTENTS

CHAPTER 1

Let's Grow Seeds!

MATERIALS

- ☐ Paper towels
- ☐ One glass jar
- ☐ 2-3 different seeds of your choice (for example, pea, kidney bean, daisy)

It is a good idea to gather your materials before you begin.

After about a week, your seed should sprout.

STEPS

1. Wet several paper towels. Wring them out to remove any extra water.
2. Crumple the paper towels into balls. There should be enough to fill the jar.

3. Place one seed of each kind along the side of the jar.

4. Place the jar near a sunny window.

5. Watch the seeds grow. After one week, all the seeds should sprout. You can draw pictures of their growth every day. Measure each plant. Compare their heights. Which grew the fastest? Which was the tallest?

See how tall your plants grow. How are they the same? How are they different?

CHAPTER 2

What Is a Seed?

A seed is a small baby plant wrapped in a hard shell. It helps the parent plant **reproduce** or make a new plant. Two kinds of plants produce seeds. **Gymnosperms** have seeds on their outside surface. They include **conifers**. Conifers produce woody cones. They have needle-shaped leaves.

Some seeds are planted into the ground by people. Others are planted by nature.

All angiosperms have ovaries. Seeds are found inside fruit because that is a plant's ovary.

Angiosperms are flowering plants. Most plants on Earth are angiosperms. Their seeds are enclosed in an **ovary**. The ovary is sometimes inside a fruit. Flowers, herbs, and many types of trees are angiosperms.

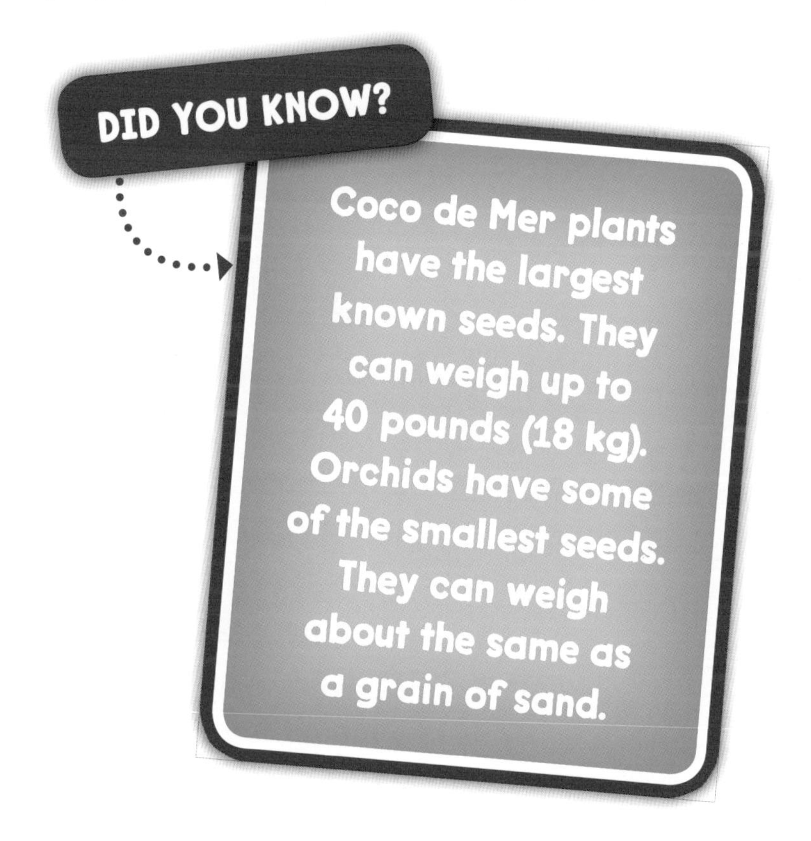

CHAPTER 3

How Does a Seed Grow?

Most plants create grains called pollen. In angiosperms, pollen sticks to insects such as bees and butterflies. They carry pollen between flowers. Gymnosperms have their pollen carried by the wind. **Pollination** is when pollen travels between plants. Plants use the pollen to make seeds and reproduce.

Pollen is carried between plants by insects such as honeybees.

INSIDE A BEAN SEED

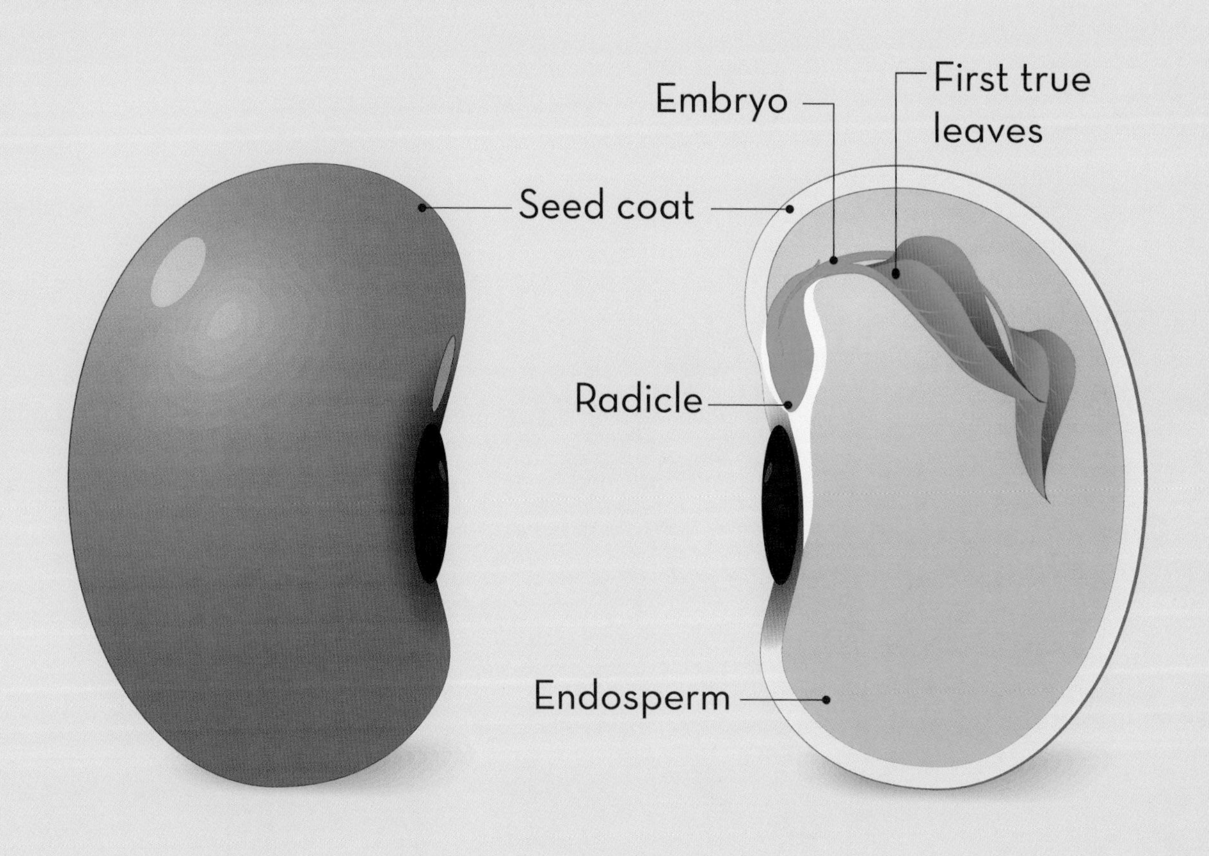

Seeds have many parts to help them grow into adult plants.

Seeds have an **embryo** and a seed coat. The embryo will eventually grow into an adult plant. The seed coat protects the embryo from extreme temperatures and insects. Most seeds have a food source called **endosperm**.

Seeds need air, water, and soil to grow. They also need the right temperature and amount of sunlight. When conditions are just right, **germination** begins. The seeds start to grow.

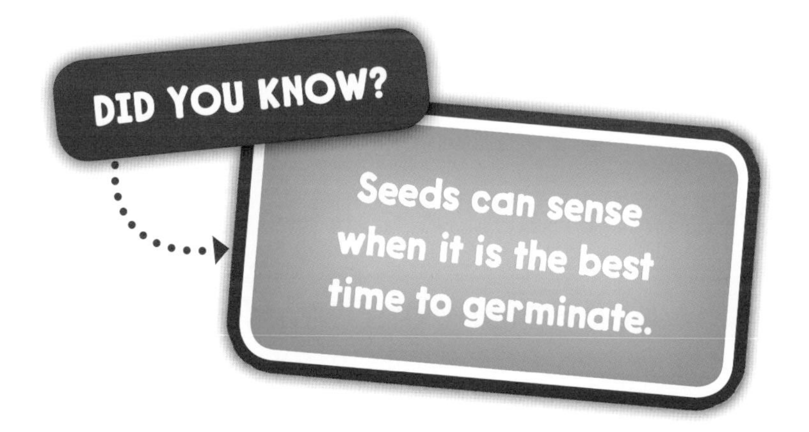

When germination begins, the seed absorbs water. The seed coat softens and swells. Next, the seed uses the endosperm to grow. Every living thing is made of tiny cells. Cells inside the seed divide. This creates new cells. The embryo grows bigger as more cells form. This helps the embryo push out of the seed coat.

A main root grows out of the bottom of the seed. This is called a radicle. The radicle anchors the seed to the ground. It helps the growing plant absorb water.

After water is absorbed, a shoot grows from the seed. Small leaves appear. The baby plant becomes a **seedling**.

A shoot grows out of the seed and becomes a seedling.

As the seedling grows, the endosperm shrinks and is used up. The seedling develops more roots. These roots help it get nutrients and water from the soil. The leaves grow. The seedling becomes a grown plant.

CHAPTER 4

How Do Seeds Travel?

Seeds help plants spread and grow in new areas. This is because seeds travel. There are many ways seeds travel. Animals eat seeds. When they pass waste, seeds are dropped in a new place. Other seeds stick to animals' fur or skin. Wind and bodies of water also carry seeds to new places. The hard seed coat protects the seed while it travels.

Dandelion seeds are carried by the wind.

Many seeds are also tasty snacks, such as pumpkin seeds.

Humans also plant seeds. Sometimes they eat seeds. They are eaten whole or used as spices. Some seeds are used to create foods and drinks. Cooking oils and coffee are made from seeds. Seeds help support life on Earth.

Glossary

angiosperms (AN-jee-uh-spurms) Angiosperms are plants with seeds in an ovary. Angiosperms are flowering plants.

conifer (KON-ih-fur) A conifer is a plant that produces woody cones. Pine trees are a type of conifer.

embryo (EM-bree-oh) An embryo is a undeveloped plant contained in a seed. An embryo grows into an adult plant.

endosperm (EN-do-spurm) Endosperm is a seed's food source. The embryo uses endosperm as food until it can make its own.

germination (jur-muh-NAY-shun) Germination is the process of developing into a plant. Germination is only possible when conditions are right.

gymnosperms (JIM-nuh-spurms) Gymnosperms are plants with seeds on their surface, not in an ovary. Conifers have seeds on its outside and are examples of gymnosperms.

ovary (OH-vuh-ree) The ovary is the part of a plant that holds seeds. Angiosperms keep their seeds inside an ovary.

pollination (pol-uh-NAY-shun) Pollination is the process of carrying pollen to a plant. Pollination is used by plants to make seeds.

reproduce (re-pro-DOOS) To reproduce is to have young or offspring. Seeds help plants reproduce.

seedling (SEED-ling) A seedling is a young plant grown from a seed. A baby plant is also called a seedling.

To Learn More

In the Library

Duke, Shirley. *Step-by-Step Experiments with Plants*. Mankato, MN: The Child's World, 2012.

Higgins, Nadia. *Experiment with What a Plant Needs to Grow*. Minneapolis, MN: Lerner Publications, 2015.

Sirett, Dawn. *I Can Grow a Flower*. New York, NY: DK Publishing, 2018.

On the Web

Visit our website for links about seeds:
childsworld.com/links

Note to Parents, Teachers, and Librarians: We routinely verify our Web links to make sure they are safe and active sites. So encourage your readers to check them out!

Index